Mastering YouTube Marketing

Strategies for Success

Alex Westwood

Disclaimer: The information provided in this book is for general informational purposes only. While every effort has been made to ensure the accuracy and completeness of the information, the author and publisher make no representations or warranties of any kind, express or implied, about the completeness, accuracy, reliability, suitability, or availability with respect to the book or the information, products, services, or related graphics contained in the book for any purpose. Any reliance you place on such information is therefore strictly at your own risk.

Limit of Liability/Disclaimer of Warranty: The author and publisher shall not be held liable for any damages arising from the use of this book or any information provided within. The inclusion of any links or recommendations in this book does not imply endorsement or guarantee the authenticity, accuracy, or reliability of the information contained within those links. Any reliance you place on such information is therefore strictly at your own risk.

Acknowledgments: The author would like to express gratitude to all those who have provided support and assistance in the creation of this book, including but not limited to editors, proofreaders, designers, and mentors.

Note: The techniques and strategies discussed in this book are based on the author's experience and research. Results may vary, and success is not guaranteed. It is recommended that readers conduct their own research and consult with professionals before implementing any marketing strategies or making business decisions.

TABLE OF CONTENTS

By following the strategies and techniques outlined in this book, you will gain the knowledge and skills to master YouTube marketing, build a loyal audience, and achieve success on the world's largest video-sharing platform. Get ready to take your brand or business to new heights with the power of YouTube!

Introduction

Welcome to "Mastering YouTube Marketing: Strategies for Success." In today's digital landscape, YouTube has emerged as a powerful platform for content creators, businesses, and individuals alike. With over two billion logged-in monthly users and one billion hours of video consumed every day, YouTube offers immense opportunities to reach and engage with a global audience.

Whether you're an aspiring YouTuber, a business looking to promote your products or services, or a marketer seeking to harness the power of video marketing, this book is your comprehensive guide to navigating the world of YouTube marketing and maximizing your success on the platform.

The Rise of YouTube and Its Impact on Online Marketing

In this chapter, we will delve into the origins of YouTube and its evolution into a dominant force in the online world. We will explore the reasons behind YouTube's popularity, its influence on consumer behavior, and the shifting landscape of online marketing in the age of video content.

Understanding the YouTube Audience and Demographics

To succeed on YouTube, it is essential to understand the platform's diverse audience. In this chapter, we will examine the demographics and viewing habits of YouTube users, enabling you to tailor your content to resonate with your target audience.

Setting Up Your YouTube Channel for Success

Creating an optimized YouTube channel is the foundation for your marketing efforts. This chapter will guide you through the process of setting up your channel, optimizing your profile, and establishing a strong brand identity that captivates your viewers.

Developing a Content Strategy for YouTube

Creating compelling and relevant content is key to attracting and retaining viewers. In this chapter, we will explore how to define your content strategy, identify your target audience, and plan engaging videos that align with your brand and goals.

Optimizing Your Videos for Maximum Visibility

To stand out amidst the vast sea of YouTube videos, you need to optimize your content for discoverability. We will discuss techniques for keyword research, crafting compelling titles and descriptions, and creating visually appealing thumbnails that entice viewers to click.

Building and Engaging Your YouTube Community

Building an engaged community is crucial for long-term success on YouTube. This chapter will explore strategies for fostering interaction, responding to comments, collaborating with other creators, and leveraging social media platforms to promote your channel and expand your reach.

Monetizing Your YouTube Channel

In this chapter, we will dive into the various methods of monetizing your YouTube channel. From advertising and sponsorships to affiliate marketing and channel memberships, we will discuss the opportunities available to generate revenue from your content.

Analyzing and Optimizing Your YouTube Performance

Measuring your performance is vital to understanding what works and what doesn't on YouTube. We will explore the analytics and insights tools provided by YouTube and discuss how to analyze data, track key metrics, and optimize your content and strategy for continued growth.

YouTube Advertising and Promotions

YouTube offers powerful advertising options to amplify your reach and promote your brand. In this chapter, we will explore different ad formats, targeting options, and strategies to ensure your advertising campaigns deliver the desired results.

YouTube Success Stories and Case Studies

Inspiration can be found in the success stories of others. This chapter will highlight compelling examples of brands, individuals, and campaigns that have achieved remarkable success on YouTube. By learning from their strategies and tactics, you can gain insights to apply to your own efforts.

Future Trends in YouTube Marketing

YouTube is constantly evolving, and staying ahead of the curve is essential for continued success. In this chapter, we will discuss emerging trends, new features, and innovative strategies that are shaping the future of YouTube marketing.

Your YouTube Marketing Journey Begins!

Chapter 1

Understanding the Power of YouTube in the Digital Landscape

1.1 The Rise of YouTube and Its Impact on Online Marketing

YouTube, founded in 2005, has revolutionized the way people consume and interact with video content. With its exponential growth and global reach, YouTube has become an influential platform that shapes popular culture and drives online engagement. This section explores the remarkable rise of YouTube and its impact on the digital landscape.

YouTube's inception marked a new era of video sharing, empowering individuals to create, upload, and share their videos with the world. As the platform gained popularity, it attracted a diverse range of content creators, from aspiring musicians to talented filmmakers, vloggers, educators, and businesses. The exponential growth of user-generated content has transformed YouTube into a vast repository of knowledge, entertainment, and inspiration.

The impact of YouTube on online marketing cannot be overstated. Traditional advertising channels faced significant disruption as YouTube offered a cost-effective and highly engaging alternative. The platform's ability to target specific demographics, combined with its massive user base, allowed businesses to reach their desired audience more effectively. Furthermore, YouTube's interactive nature enabled viewers to engage with content through comments, likes, shares, and subscriptions, fostering a sense of community and brand loyalty.

1.2 The Benefits of YouTube Marketing for Businesses

YouTube marketing offers a multitude of benefits for businesses seeking to establish their online presence, build brand awareness, and drive customer engagement. This section explores the advantages that YouTube provides as a marketing platform.

Firstly, YouTube provides an opportunity to showcase products or services through visually compelling and engaging videos. Unlike text-based advertisements, videos allow businesses to convey their message more effectively, capturing the attention of their target audience and leaving a lasting impression. From product demonstrations and tutorials to testimonials and brand storytelling, the versatility of video content on YouTube enables businesses to connect with their customers on a deeper level.

Secondly, YouTube's vast user base offers businesses an immense potential reach. With billions of monthly active users and countless hours of video watched daily, YouTube provides a platform to connect with a global audience. By optimizing their videos for search engine visibility and utilizing effective promotional strategies, businesses can leverage YouTube's reach to attract new customers and expand their market presence.

Additionally, YouTube's analytics and insights tools provide businesses with valuable data to measure the performance of their videos and optimize their marketing strategies. Detailed metrics such as views, watch time, engagement rates, and audience demographics help businesses understand their target audience better and refine their content to meet their preferences and needs.

1.3 Exploring YouTube's Features and User Demographics

YouTube offers a wide range of features that enhance the user experience and provide businesses with various tools for effective marketing. Understanding these features and the demographics of YouTube users is essential for creating targeted and engaging content.

YouTube's features include video monetization options, community engagement tools, live streaming capabilities, and interactive elements such as annotations, cards, and end screens. Each feature presents opportunities for businesses to enhance their videos, drive viewer engagement, and promote their brand or products effectively.

When it comes to user demographics, YouTube boasts a diverse audience spanning various age groups, interests, and geographic locations. Understanding the demographics of YouTube users allows businesses to tailor their content and marketing strategies to resonate with their target audience effectively. By analyzing viewer data and trends, businesses can gain insights into the preferences, behaviors, and interests of their audience, enabling them to deliver content that aligns with their expectations.

In conclusion, YouTube's rise to prominence has had a profound impact on the digital landscape. Its influence on online marketing is undeniable, offering businesses a platform to reach a global audience, engage with customers through visually compelling videos, and leverage powerful analytics to optimize their marketing efforts. By understanding YouTube's features, benefits, and user demographics, businesses can harness the power ofthis platform to drive their marketing success and thrive in the digital age.

Chapter 2

Setting Up Your YouTube Channel

2.1 Creating a Channel and Optimizing Your Profile

Setting up a YouTube channel is the first step towards establishing your presence on the platform. In this section, we will guide you through the process of creating a channel and optimizing your profile for maximum impact.

To create a YouTube channel, you will need a Google account. Once you have signed in to your Google account, visit the YouTube website and click on the "Create a Channel" option. You will be prompted to choose a name for your channel, which should align with your brand or the content you plan to share.

After creating your channel, it's time to optimize your profile. Start by uploading a profile picture that represents your brand or yourself as a content creator. This image will be displayed next to your videos and comments, so choose a clear and recognizable image that reflects your brand identity.

Next, customize your channel layout by adding a channel banner or cover art. This banner is a prominent visual element that appears at the top of your channel page, so it's essential to design something eye-catching and representative of your brand. Consider using professional graphics, logos, or high-quality images that convey your channel's theme or message.

2.2 Designing Compelling Channel Art and Thumbnails

Compelling channel art and thumbnails play a crucial role in attracting viewers and encouraging them to click on your videos. Channel art refers to the visual elements that appear on your channel's homepage, while thumbnails are the small images that represent each video.

When designing channel art, consider the dimensions and guidelines provided by YouTube to ensure it displays correctly across different devices. Use this space to convey your channel's branding, showcase your content, or highlight upcoming videos. Incorporate visually appealing images, compelling text, and consistent design elements to create a cohesive and professional look.

Thumbnails, on the other hand, should entice viewers to click on your videos. They should be visually captivating, relevant to the video's content, and optimized for readability. Consider using high-quality images, bold typography, and contrasting colors to make your thumbnails stand out in search results and recommended videos sections.

2.3 Crafting an Engaging Channel Description and About Section

Your channel description and about section provide an opportunity to introduce your brand, tell your story, and engage with your audience. Craft these sections carefully to create a compelling narrative and entice viewers to subscribe to your channel.

In your channel description, provide a concise overview of your channel's content and value proposition. Explain what viewers can expect from your videos, the topics you cover, and why they should subscribe. Use this space to showcase your expertise, unique selling points, or the entertainment value you provide.

The about section allows you to delve deeper into your brand or personal background. Share your story, your passion for creating content, and any relevant achievements or credentials. Consider including links to your website, social media accounts, or other channels where viewers can connect with you further.

Additionally, optimize your channel description and about section with relevant keywords that align with your content and target audience. This will help improve your visibility in search results and attract viewers who are interested in your niche.

In conclusion, setting up your YouTube channel is a critical step towards establishing your presence on the platform. By creating a channel, optimizing your profile, designing compelling channel art and thumbnails, and crafting an engaging channel description and about section, you lay the foundation for attracting viewers and building a loyal subscriber base. A well-optimized channel not only enhances your brand's credibility but also increases the chances of your videos being discovered by a wider audience.

Remember that consistency and branding are key when setting up your YouTube channel. Use the same profile picture, channel art style, and color palette across all your branding elements to create a cohesive and recognizable identity. This will help viewers associate your content with your brand, making it easier for them to find and engage with your channel.

Furthermore, regularly update your channel art and thumbnails to reflect new videos, series, or promotional campaigns. Keeping your visuals fresh and relevant ensures that viewers are enticed to click on your videos and explore your content further.

In addition to visual elements, it's important to optimize the metadata associated with your channel. This includes your channel name, video titles, descriptions, and tags. Conduct keyword research to identify the most relevant and popular search terms in your niche, and incorporate them strategically in your metadata. This will improve the visibility of your videos in YouTube's search results and increase the likelihood of attracting organic traffic.

Lastly, make sure to enable the "Customize the layout of your channel" option in your YouTube settings. This will allow you to arrange your channel's sections, such as playlists, featured videos, and social media links, in a way that suits your content strategy and user experience goals.

By setting up your YouTube channel thoughtfully and optimizing its profile, visuals, and metadata, you lay a strong foundation for success. Remember to regularly review and update your channel's branding and metadata as your content evolves and your audience grows. With a well-structured and appealing channel, you increase your chances of capturing viewers' attention, engaging them with your content, and ultimately growing your YouTube presence.

Chapter 3

Developing a Content Strategy for YouTube

3.1 Defining Your Brand Identity and Voice

Before diving into creating content for your YouTube channel, it's crucial to define your brand identity and voice. Your brand identity encompasses the essence of your brand, including its values, mission, and unique selling proposition. Your brand voice, on the other hand, refers to the tone and style of your communication.

Take some time to identify what sets your brand apart from others in your niche. What makes your content unique? What values do you want to convey to your audience? Understanding your brand identity will help you create content that aligns with your overall brand strategy and resonates with your target audience.

Once you have a clear brand identity, define your brand voice. Is it casual and conversational? Professional and informative? Fun and entertaining? Determine the tone that best reflects your brand and appeals to your target audience. Consistency in your brand voice will help build familiarity and trust with your viewers.

3.2 Identifying Your Target Audience on YouTube

To create content that resonates with your audience, you need to understand who your target audience is. Start by conducting research to identify the demographics, interests, and preferences of your ideal viewers. This will help you tailor your content to their needs and preferences.

Use YouTube Analytics to gain insights into your existing audience. Analyze the demographics, watch time, and engagement metrics of your viewers. This data will give you a better understanding of who is already watching your content and help you identify any gaps or opportunities.

Additionally, conduct keyword research related to your niche to understand what your target audience is searching for on YouTube. Tools like Google Trends and YouTube's search autocomplete feature can provide valuable insights into popular search terms and topics. Use this information to guide your content creation and ensure that you are addressing the needs and interests of your target audience.

3.3 Planning and Creating High-Quality Video Content

Once you have defined your brand identity and identified your target audience, it's time to plan and create high-quality video content. Start by brainstorming video ideas that align with your brand and cater to the interests of your target audience. Consider the types of content that perform well in your niche and how you can put your unique spin on them.

Create a content calendar to help you stay organized and consistent with your uploads. This will ensure that you consistently deliver fresh and engaging content to your audience. Plan your videos in advance, including the topics, formats, and any supporting materials or resources you may need.

When it comes to creating your videos, invest in quality equipment, including a good camera, microphone, and lighting setup. While you don't need professional-grade equipment starting out, ensure that your videos are visually and audibly clear and appealing to your viewers.

Focus on providing value to your audience with each video. Whether it's educational, entertaining, or inspiring, make sure your content addresses a specific need or interest of your viewers. Be authentic and genuine in your delivery, as this will help you connect with your audience on a deeper level.

3.4 Utilizing YouTube's Video Formats and Features

YouTube offers various video formats and features that can enhance the engagement and visibility of your content. Familiarize yourself with these formats and features to make the most out of your YouTube strategy.

- Standard videos: These are the most common video format on YouTube, where you upload and share your content with your audience. Experiment with different video lengths, ranging from short-form content to longer, in-depth videos, based on your audience preferences and the nature of your content.

- Live videos: YouTube's live streaming feature allows you to interact with your audience in real-time. Consider hosting live Q&A sessions, product launches, or behind-the-scenes content to engage with your viewers and build a sense of community.

- Shorts: YouTube Shorts are short-form vertical videos that can be up to 60 seconds long. These bite-sized videos are designed to capture viewers' attention quickly and are ideal for creating snackable content that is easily consumable and shareable.

- Community posts: YouTube's community tab allows you to engage with your audience through text-based posts, polls, and images. Use this feature to share updates, ask for feedback, or create a sense of exclusivity for your subscribers.

- Cards and end screens: These interactive elements can be added to your videos to encourage viewers to take specific actions, such as subscribing to your channel, watching related videos, or visiting your website. Use cards and end screens strategically to promote your content and engage your audience further.

As you develop your content strategy, consider how you can leverage these video formats and features to enhance viewer engagement, attract new subscribers, and increase the visibility of your channel.

By understanding the importance of defining your brand identity and voice, identifying your target audience, planning and creating high-quality content, and utilizing YouTube's video formats and features, you will be well on your way to mastering YouTube marketing and achieving success on the platform. Remember to consistently evaluate and refine your content strategy based on audience feedback and evolving trends in the digital landscape.

Chapter 4

Optimizing Your Videos for Maximum Visibility

4.1 Keyword Research and SEO for YouTube

Keyword research and search engine optimization (SEO) play a crucial role in ensuring that your videos are discoverable on YouTube. By understanding the keywords and search terms your target audience uses, you can optimize your videos to appear in relevant search results.

Start by brainstorming a list of keywords related to your video topic. Consider the terms that your target audience is likely to use when searching for content like yours. Use keyword research tools like Google Keyword Planner, YouTube's search autocomplete feature, and third-party tools like TubeBuddy and VidIQ to gather data on search volume and competition for different keywords.

When selecting keywords, aim for a balance between popularity and competitiveness. Targeting highly popular keywords may result in fierce competition, making it difficult for your videos to rank. On the other hand, targeting less competitive keywords may result in lower search volume. Find a sweet spot where you can optimize your videos for relevant keywords with a reasonable level of competition.

Incorporate your chosen keywords strategically throughout your video's metadata, including the title, description, tags, and video transcript. Use your primary keyword in the video title to make it clear to viewers and YouTube's algorithm what your video is about. In the description, provide a detailed overview of your video's content, incorporating relevant keywords naturally. Remember to also include additional related keywords as tags to further optimize your video's visibility.

4.2 Crafting Attention-Grabbing Titles and Descriptions

Titles and descriptions play a crucial role in capturing viewers' attention and convincing them to click on your video. Craft attention-grabbing titles that accurately represent the content of your video while piquing curiosity. Consider using numbers, compelling adjectives, or posing questions to make your titles more enticing.

In the video description, provide a detailed summary of your video's content. Use this opportunity to include relevant keywords naturally, as well as links to relevant resources, social media profiles, or products mentioned in the video. You can also include timestamps for different sections of your video, making it easier for viewers to navigate and find specific information.

Remember to make your descriptions viewer-friendly by breaking up the text into paragraphs and using bullet points or lists when appropriate. Use the first few lines of your description to provide a compelling teaser that hooks viewers and encourages them to continue reading and watching.

4.3 Creating Compelling Thumbnails and Custom Video End Screens

Thumbnails are the first visual impression viewers have of your video, and they can greatly influence whether someone decides to click and watch. Create compelling thumbnails that are visually appealing, relevant to your video's content, and stand out from the crowd. Use high-resolution images, bold typography, and vibrant colors to capture viewers' attention.

Consider using custom video end screens to promote additional content and encourage viewers to take specific actions. End screens are interactive elements that appear in the final moments of your video and can include links to subscribe, watch related videos, or visit your website. Design end screens that are visually appealing, clearly communicate the desired actions, and align with your brand's visual identity.

Experiment with different thumbnail designs and end screen layouts to find what works best for your audience. Monitor the click-through rates and audience retention metrics to identify which thumbnails and end screens are most effective at engaging your viewers.

4.4 Enhancing Video Engagement with Cards, Annotations, and Playlists

YouTube offers various features that can enhance viewer engagement and drive them to explore more of your content. Take advantage of these features to keep viewers engaged and encourage them to take specific actions.

Cards are interactive elements that can be added to your videos to promote other videos, playlists, websites, or merchandise. Use cards strategically to cross-promote relevant content or products and keep viewers within your YouTube ecosystem.

Annotations are text overlays that can be added to your videos, providing additional information or calls to action. However, note that annotations are no longer supported on mobile devices, so consider using cards or end screens as alternatives for mobile viewers.

Create playlists to organize your videos thematically or chronologically. Playlists make it easier for viewers to navigate through your content and binge-watch related videos. Curate your playlists thoughtfully to provide a seamless viewing experience and encourage viewers to spend more time on your channel.

Regularly evaluate the performance of your video optimizations and engagement features. Monitor metrics like watch time, click-through rates, and audience retention to identify areas for improvement. Experiment with different strategies, such as testing different titles, thumbnails, or engagement elements, and use the data to refine your approach.

By optimizing your videos for maximum visibility through keyword research and SEO, crafting attention-grabbing titles and descriptions, creating compelling thumbnails and custom video end screens, and enhancing engagement with cards, annotations, and playlists, you can increase the discoverability and viewer engagement of your YouTube content. Stay tuned for the next chapter, where we'll dive deeper into audience growth and community building strategies on YouTube.

Chapter 5

Building and Engaging Your YouTube Community

5.1 Encouraging Viewer Engagement and Interaction

Building a strong community of engaged viewers is key to the success of your YouTube channel. Encouraging viewer engagement and interaction can help foster a sense of connection and loyalty among your audience. Here are some strategies to encourage engagement:

- Ask for feedback: Encourage viewers to leave comments and share their thoughts on your videos. Ask specific questions or invite them to share their own experiences related to the video's topic.

- Respond to comments: Take the time to respond to comments on your videos. Show appreciation for positive feedback, address concerns, and engage in conversations with your viewers. This interaction helps build relationships and encourages viewers to continue engaging with your content.

- Conduct polls and surveys: Use YouTube's community tab or external polling tools to gather feedback and opinions from your audience. Polls and surveys not only encourage engagement but also provide valuable insights into your audience's preferences and interests.

- Create interactive content: Incorporate interactive elements into your videos, such as quizzes, challenges, or interactive annotations. These elements encourage viewers to actively participate in the content and create a more immersive experience.

5.2 Responding to Comments and Building Relationships

Responding to comments is an essential part of building and nurturing your YouTube community. It shows that you value your viewers' opinions and are actively engaged with them. Here are some tips for managing and responding to comments effectively:

- Regularly monitor and moderate comments: Keep an eye on the comments section of your videos and ensure that the conversation remains respectful and on-topic. Remove any spam or inappropriate comments to maintain a positive environment.

- Reply to comments in a timely manner: Aim to respond to comments as soon as possible. This shows your viewers that you are actively engaged and interested in their feedback. Even a simple "thank you" or "like" can go a long way in building rapport.

- Encourage meaningful discussions: Foster a sense of community by asking follow-up questions or sparking conversations within the comment section. This can encourage viewers to engage with each other and create a vibrant community around your channel.

- Consider featuring viewer comments: Highlight exceptional or insightful comments in your videos or community posts. This not only acknowledges your viewers but also encourages others to participate in the discussion.

Building relationships with your audience takes time and effort, but the payoff is a loyal and engaged community that will support and advocate for your channel.

5.3 Collaborating with Other YouTubers and Influencers

Collaborating with other YouTubers and influencers can be a powerful strategy for growing your audience and expanding your reach. Here's how you can approach collaborations:

- Find relevant creators: Look for YouTubers or influencers who create content that aligns with your niche or complements your own content. Consider their audience size and engagement levels to find potential collaborators who can benefit both parties.

- Reach out with a clear proposition: When reaching out to potential collaborators, be specific about your ideas and the potential benefits for both parties. Highlight what makes your collaboration unique and why it would be valuable to their audience.

- Collaborate on content creation: Explore opportunities to create videos together, such as joint Q&A sessions, challenge videos, or guest appearances. This allows you to tap into each other's audience and expose your content to new viewers.

- Cross-promote each other's channels: Collaborate on promotional activities, such as featuring each other's channels in video shout-outs, end screens, or community posts. This cross-promotion helps drive traffic and subscribers to both channels.

Remember to approach collaborations with authenticity and a genuine desire to create valuable content for your audience. Building relationships with other creators can open doors to new opportunities and help you tap into new audiences.

5.4 Promoting Your YouTube

- Channel on Other Platforms: Promoting your YouTube channel on other platforms can help drive traffic, increase visibility, and attract new viewers. Here are some effective strategies for cross-promotion:

- Leverage social media: Share teasers, snippets, or behind-the-scenes content from your YouTube videos on platforms like Instagram, Twitter, or Facebook. Encourage your followers to check out the full video on your YouTube channel.

- Collaborate with bloggers and websites: Reach out to relevant bloggers or websites in your niche and offer to create guest posts or provide valuable content that links back to your YouTube channel. This can help you tap into their audience and drive traffic to your videos.

- Utilize email marketing: If you have an email list, regularly promote your YouTube videos to your subscribers. Create compelling newsletters or updates that highlight your latest video releases and encourage your subscribers to watch, comment, and share.

- Participate in online communities: Engage in online forums, groups, or communities related to your niche. Provide valuable insights and advice, and when appropriate, share links to your YouTube videos that offer further information or support.

- Collaborate with brands and influencers: Partner with brands or influencers in your industry to create sponsored content or product reviews that feature your YouTube channel. This can help expose your channel to their audience and attract new viewers.

When promoting your YouTube channel on other platforms, it's important to focus on providing value and building genuine connections. Avoid spammy or overly promotional tactics that may alienate potential viewers.

By implementing these strategies, you can effectively build and engage your YouTube community, fostering a loyal audience that actively participates in discussions, collaborates with other creators, and helps promote your channel. In the next chapter, we'll delve into strategies for monetizing your YouTube channel and turning your passion into a profitable venture.

Chapter 6

Monetizing Your YouTube Channel

6.1 Understanding YouTube's Monetization Policies and Requirements

Before you can start monetizing your YouTube channel, it's important to understand YouTube's monetization policies and meet the requirements set by the platform. YouTube has specific guidelines in place to ensure that channels meet certain criteria before they can monetize their content. Here are some key points to consider:

- YouTube Partner Program: To be eligible for monetization, you need to join the YouTube Partner Program. This program enables you to earn money from ads, channel memberships, and other monetization features.

- Minimum requirements: YouTube has set minimum requirements that channels need to meet to be considered for monetization. These requirements include having at least 1,000 subscribers and 4,000 watch hours in the past 12 months.

- Advertiser-friendly content: YouTube has guidelines on the type of content that can be monetized. It's important to create content that is compliant with YouTube's advertiser-friendly policies to ensure that your videos are eligible for ads.

6.2 Implementing Ads and Sponsorships

Ads are one of the primary ways to monetize your YouTube channel. YouTube offers different types of ads that you can implement to generate revenue. Here are some common ad formats:

- Pre-roll ads: These are ads that play before your video starts. You earn revenue based on the number of ad views or clicks.

- Mid-roll ads: These are ads that appear in the middle of your video. They interrupt the viewing experience but can generate higher revenue compared to pre-roll ads.

- Overlay ads: These are semi-transparent ads that appear at the bottom of your video. They can be banner ads or text ads and don't interrupt the viewing experience.

In addition to ads, sponsorships can be a lucrative way to monetize your YouTube channel. Collaborating with brands or companies that align with your content and audience can lead to sponsored videos or product placements. However, it's important to maintain transparency and disclose any sponsored content to your viewers.

6.3 Exploring Affiliate Marketing and Product Promotions

Affiliate marketing involves promoting products or services and earning a commission for each sale or referral generated through your unique affiliate link. It can be a highly profitable monetization strategy for YouTube channels. Here's how you can leverage affiliate marketing:

- Choose relevant affiliate programs: Select affiliate programs that align with your niche and audience. Look for products or services that you genuinely believe in and that your viewers would find valuable.

- Incorporate affiliate links strategically: Place affiliate links in your video descriptions, end screens, or within the video content itself. Provide genuine recommendations and highlight the benefits of the products or services you're promoting.

- Track performance and optimize: Use affiliate tracking tools to monitor the performance of your affiliate links. Analyze which products or promotions are generating the most conversions and optimize your strategies accordingly.

Product promotions can also be a source of revenue. You can create your own merchandise, such as branded merchandise or digital products, and promote them to your audience. This allows you to monetize your channel while also building your brand.

6.4 Leveraging YouTube Memberships and Crowdfunding

YouTube offers a membership feature that allows your viewers to become channel members by paying a monthly fee. In return, members gain access to exclusive perks, such as badges, emojis, or members-only content. This membership model can provide a consistent source of revenue and strengthen the connection with your most dedicated fans.

Crowdfunding is another option for monetizing your YouTube channel. Platforms like Patreon or Kickstarter allow you to receive direct financial support from your viewers. You can offer special rewards or incentives to those who contribute to your crowdfunding campaign, such as exclusive content or personalized shout-outs.

It's important to provide value to your members or supporters and keep them engaged.

Regularly communicate with your members, offer exclusive content, and show appreciation for their support.

By implementing these monetization strategies, you can turn your YouTube channel into a profitable venture while continuing to provide valuable content to your audience. In the next chapter, we'll explore strategies for expanding your reach and growing your YouTube channel.

Chapter 7

Analyzing and Optimizing Your YouTube Performance

7.1 Utilizing YouTube Analytics for Insights and Metrics

YouTube Analytics provides valuable data and metrics that can help you understand how your channel and videos are performing. By analyzing these insights, you can make informed decisions and optimize your YouTube strategy. Here are some key metrics and features to consider:

- Views and Watch Time: These metrics indicate how many people have watched your videos and how much time they've spent watching. Pay attention to the watch time, as it is an important factor in YouTube's algorithm.

- Audience Demographics: YouTube Analytics provides information about your audience's age, gender, and geographic location. Understanding your audience demographics can help you tailor your content to their preferences and interests.

- Traffic Sources: YouTube Analytics shows you where your viewers are coming from, such as YouTube search, suggested videos, or external websites. This information can help you identify effective promotional channels and optimize your marketing efforts.

7.2 Tracking Video Performance and Audience Engagement

In addition to overall channel metrics, it's important to track the performance of individual videos. This can help you identify which videos are resonating with your audience and which ones may need improvement. Here are some metrics to focus on:

- Average View Duration: This metric measures the average time viewers spend watching your videos. It can help you gauge the effectiveness of your content and identify areas for improvement.

- Audience Retention: Audience retention shows the percentage of viewers who continue watching your video at each moment. By analyzing audience retention data, you can identify which parts of your videos are engaging and which parts may be causing viewers to drop off.

- Likes, Dislikes, and Comments: Pay attention to the engagement metrics, such as likes, dislikes, and comments. These metrics indicate how viewers are responding to your content and can provide valuable feedback.

- Click-through Rate (CTR): CTR measures the percentage of viewers who click on your video after seeing it in search results or as a suggested video. A higher CTR indicates that your video is compelling and attracting viewers' attention.

7.3 A/B Testing and Experimenting with Different Strategies

To continuously improve your YouTube performance, it's important to experiment with different strategies and A/B test your content. Here are some ideas to consider:

- Video Titles and Thumbnails: Test different titles and thumbnails to see which ones attract more clicks and views. Optimize your titles and thumbnails to be compelling, visually appealing, and aligned with the content.

- Video Length and Format: Experiment with different video lengths and formats to see what resonates best with your audience. Some viewers prefer short, concise videos, while others prefer longer, more in-depth content.

- Content Topics and Styles: Test different topics and content styles to identify which ones generate the most engagement and interest. Pay attention to the feedback from your audience and adjust your content strategy accordingly.

7.4 Optimizing Your YouTube Channel for Growth and Success

To maximize your YouTube success, optimize your channel to attract new viewers and retain existing ones. Here are some optimization tips:

- Channel Keywords and Descriptions: Use relevant keywords in your channel description and metadata to improve your visibility in YouTube search results.

- Playlists and Channel Organization: Create playlists to organize your videos and make it easier for viewers to navigate your content. This can improve the overall user experience and encourage viewers to watch more of your videos.

- Channel Trailer: Create a compelling channel trailer that introduces new viewers to your content and encourages them to subscribe.

- Collaborations and Cross-Promotion: Collaborate with other YouTubers or influencers in your niche to expand your reach and attract new viewers. Cross-promote each other's channels or create joint content to tap into each other's audiences.

By analyzing your YouTube performance, experimenting with different strategies, and optimizing your channel, you can continually improve your presence on the platform and drive growth and success for your YouTube marketing efforts.

In the next chapter, we'll explore advanced YouTube marketing strategies and techniques that can take your channel to the next level.

Chapter 8

YouTube Advertising and Paid Promotions

8.1 Introduction to YouTube Ads and Ad Formats

YouTube offers various advertising options to help businesses reach a wider audience and promote their products or services. Understanding the different ad formats and their benefits can significantly enhance your marketing efforts. Here are some common YouTube ad formats:

- TrueView Ads: TrueView ads are skippable video ads that appear before, during, or after YouTube videos. Viewers have the option to skip the ad after a few seconds, making it a more user-friendly format. You only pay when viewers watch your ad for at least 30 seconds or engage with it.

- Non-Skippable In-Stream Ads: Non-skippable in-stream ads are video ads that viewers must watch in their entirety before accessing the desired content. While they offer higher visibility, they may be seen as intrusive by some viewers.

- Bumper Ads: Bumper ads are short, non-skippable video ads that appear before YouTube videos. They have a maximum duration of six seconds and are designed to deliver concise and impactful messages.

- Display Ads: Display ads are banner ads that appear on the right side of the YouTube watch page or as overlays on the video. They can include images, text, and even interactive elements.

8.2 Creating Effective Ad Campaigns and Targeting Specific Audiences

To maximize the impact of your YouTube ads, it's essential to create effective campaigns and target specific audiences. Here are some strategies to consider:

- Define Your Ad Objectives: Clearly define the goals of your ad campaign. Whether it's brand awareness, lead generation, or driving sales, understanding your objectives will help you create targeted and impactful ads.

- Audience Targeting: Leverage YouTube's robust targeting options to reach the right audience. You can target viewers based on demographics, interests, behavior, and even specific YouTube channels.

- Ad Creative and Messaging: Develop compelling ad creative and messaging that resonates with your target audience. Focus on capturing attention within the first few seconds and delivering a clear and concise message that encourages viewers to take action.

- Call-to-Action (CTA): Include a strong and relevant call-to-action in your ads. Encourage viewers to visit your website, subscribe to your channel, make a purchase, or engage with your brand in some way.

8.3 Analyzing Ad Performance and ROI

Measuring the performance of your YouTube ads is crucial to understanding their effectiveness and optimizing future campaigns. Here are some metrics to consider:

- View Count: Track the number of views your ads receive to gauge their reach and visibility.

- View-through Rate (VTR): VTR measures the percentage of viewers who watched your ad in its entirety or up to 30 seconds. A higher VTR indicates that your ad is engaging and capturing viewers' attention.

- Click-through Rate (CTR): CTR measures the percentage of viewers who clicked on your ad after seeing it. A higher CTR indicates that your ad is compelling and driving engagement.

- Conversion Tracking: Set up conversion tracking to measure the actions viewers take after watching your ad, such as making a purchase, subscribing, or filling out a form. This allows you to determine the return on investment (ROI) of your ad campaigns.

8.4 Leveraging YouTube Influencer Marketing

In addition to running ads directly on YouTube, you can leverage YouTube influencer marketing to reach a highly engaged audience. Collaborating with popular YouTubers in your niche can amplify your brand's visibility and credibility. Here are some steps to consider when implementing influencer marketing:

- Identify Relevant Influencers: Research and identify influencers whose audience aligns with your target market. Look for influencers with a substantial following and high engagement rates.

- Establish Authentic Partnerships: Approach influencers with genuine interest in their content and a clear understanding of how your brand can add value to their audience. Develop mutually beneficial partnerships that result in authentic and engaging collaborations.

- Sponsored Content: Work with influencers to create sponsored content that integrates your brand naturally. Whether it's product reviews, tutorials, or sponsored shout-outs, the content should resonate with the influencer's audience while effectively promoting your brand.

- Track Performance: Monitor the performance of your influencer collaborations using unique tracking links, promo codes, or dedicated landing pages. This allows you to measure the impact and return on investment of each partnership.

In conclusion, YouTube advertising and influencer marketing can significantly boost your brand's visibility and engagement on the platform. By creating compelling ad campaigns, targeting specific audiences, analyzing performance metrics, and leveraging influencer partnerships, you can optimize your YouTube marketing strategy and drive meaningful results for your business.

In the next chapter, we'll explore advanced YouTube strategies and techniques to take your channel to new heights.

Chapter 9

YouTube Success Stories and Case Studies

9.1 Inspiring Examples of Brands and Individuals that Mastered YouTube Marketing

YouTube has become a powerful platform for brands and individuals to showcase their creativity, build communities, and achieve remarkable success. By examining the strategies and approaches of those who have mastered YouTube marketing, we can gain valuable insights and inspiration for our own campaigns. Here are a few examples of brands and individuals that have excelled on YouTube:

1. Red Bull: Red Bull is known for its captivating and adrenaline-pumping content on YouTube. Their videos feature extreme sports, stunts, and adventures, capturing the attention of their target audience of thrill-seekers. By consistently producing high-quality and shareable content, Red Bull has built a loyal following and generated millions of views and engagements.

2. Tasty: Tasty, a food and recipe brand owned by BuzzFeed, has mastered the art of creating short and visually appealing recipe videos. With their innovative overhead camera shots, quick editing, and easy-to-follow instructions, Tasty has become a go-to source for food inspiration on YouTube. Their videos have gone viral, generating millions of views and shares, and driving traffic to their website.

3. Casey Neistat: Casey Neistat is a renowned YouTuber who gained popularity through his vlogs and unique storytelling style. He has mastered the art of captivating his audience by sharing his daily life adventures, travel experiences, and personal insights. Neistat's authentic and relatable content has earned him a dedicated following and numerous brand collaborations.

9.2 Learning from Successful YouTube Campaigns and Strategies

Successful YouTube campaigns and strategies can provide valuable lessons and insights for marketers looking to achieve similar results. By examining these case studies, we can identify common themes and strategies that contribute to their success. Here are a few key areas to explore:

1. Content Consistency: Consistently producing high-quality and relevant content is essential for building an engaged audience. Successful YouTubers and brands maintain a regular upload schedule and deliver content that aligns with their audience's interests and preferences.

2. Audience Engagement: Engaging with the audience is crucial for building a loyal community. Successful creators respond to comments, ask for viewer feedback, and incorporate audience suggestions into their content. This interaction fosters a sense of belonging and encourages viewers to become active participants in the channel's growth.

3. Collaboration and Cross-Promotion: Collaborating with other YouTubers or influencers in the same niche can expand your reach and introduce your channel to new audiences. Successful collaborations leverage the strengths and audiences of both parties to create mutually beneficial content.

9.3 Analyzing Different Approaches for Various Goals

Different goals require different approaches on YouTube. Whether your objective is to increase brand awareness, drive website traffic, or generate sales, understanding the strategies that align with your goals is essential. Here are a few examples:

1. Brand Awareness: For brand awareness, focus on creating visually compelling and shareable content that showcases your brand's unique personality and values. Consider collaborations with influencers or running ads to extend your reach and expose your brand to a broader audience.

2. Website Traffic: To drive traffic to your website, optimize your video descriptions with relevant keywords and include calls-to-action that direct viewers to your website. You can also create tutorial or educational content that encourages viewers to visit your website for additional resources or information.

3. Sales and Conversions: To generate sales, create product-focused videos that highlight the benefits and features of your offerings. Include links in your video

descriptions or utilize YouTube's end screens and cards to direct viewers to a landing page where they can make a purchase.

By analyzing different approaches and case studies, you can identify strategies that align with your goals and apply them to your own YouTube marketing efforts.

In the next chapter, we will explore advanced techniques and strategies to further optimize your YouTube channel and take your success to the next level.

Chapter 10

Future Trends in YouTube Marketing

10.1 The Evolving Landscape of YouTube Features and Trends

YouTube is constantly evolving, introducing new features and trends that shape the way content creators and marketers engage with their audience. Staying up to date with these changes is crucial for maintaining a competitive edge. Here are some of the key trends and features shaping the future of YouTube marketing:

1. Live Streaming: Live streaming has become increasingly popular on YouTube, allowing creators to interact with their audience in real-time. Live streams provide an opportunity for engaging Q&A sessions, behind-the-scenes glimpses, product launches, and virtual events. As live streaming continues to gain traction, incorporating it into your YouTube marketing strategy can help you foster a deeper connection with your audience.

2. Short-Form Videos: Short-form videos have gained significant popularity on various social media platforms,

and YouTube is no exception. The introduction of YouTube Shorts, the platform's response to the rise of short-form video content, has opened new opportunities for creators to capture attention in a concise and engaging format. As the demand for quick and digestible content grows, incorporating short-form videos into your YouTube strategy can help you stay relevant and cater to changing viewer preferences.

3. YouTube Premium: YouTube Premium offers an ad-free viewing experience, access to exclusive content, and the ability to download videos for offline viewing. As more viewers subscribe to YouTube Premium, creators and marketers need to consider the impact of ad-free viewing on their monetization strategies. Exploring partnerships with YouTube Premium or creating exclusive content for subscribers can be a way to adapt to this evolving trend.

10.2 Embracing New Technologies and Video Formats

As technology advances, new opportunities arise for content creators and marketers to innovate and captivate their audience. Embracing new technologies and video formats can give you a competitive edge and enhance your YouTube marketing efforts. Here are a few examples:

1. Virtual Reality (VR) and Augmented Reality (AR): VR and AR technologies are transforming the way viewers engage with content. From immersive 360-degree videos to AR-enhanced experiences, incorporating these technologies into your YouTube videos can provide a unique and interactive viewing experience. Brands can leverage VR and AR to showcase products, create virtual tours, or enhance storytelling.

2. Interactive Videos: Interactive videos allow viewers to actively participate in the content by making choices or engaging with clickable elements. These videos create a more personalized and engaging experience, increasing viewer retention and interaction. By incorporating interactive elements such as quizzes, polls, or clickable annotations, you can enhance viewer engagement and create memorable experiences.

3. Vertical Video: With the rise of mobile usage, vertical video has gained popularity. Creating content optimized for vertical viewing allows for a seamless viewing experience on mobile devices. Vertical videos are especially relevant for platforms like TikTok and Instagram's IGTV. By adapting your content to the vertical format, you can tap into the growing mobile

audience and optimize your videos for social media sharing.

10.3 Staying Ahead in the Dynamic World of YouTube Marketing

To stay ahead in the dynamic world of YouTube marketing, it's essential to continuously adapt and innovate. Here are some strategies to help you navigate the evolving landscape:

1. Stay Updated: Keep a pulse on YouTube's latest updates, features, and algorithm changes. Subscribe to YouTube's official channels, attend industry events, and follow thought leaders in the YouTube marketing space to stay informed and gain insights into emerging trends.

2. Experiment and Test: Don't be afraid to try new strategies and techniques. Experiment with different content formats, video lengths, and promotional tactics to identify what resonates with your audience. A/B testing can help you refine your approach and optimize your content for maximum engagement.

3. Foster Community Engagement: Building a strong community around your channel is key to long-term success. Enc

ourage viewers to leave comments, respond to their feedback, and foster a sense of belonging. Hosting live streams, Q&A sessions, or community challenges can help strengthen the bond with your audience and foster a loyal following.

4. Collaborate and Network: Collaborating with other YouTubers or influencers in your niche can expand your reach and introduce your content to new audiences. Look for opportunities to collaborate on joint projects, guest appearances, or cross-promotion to tap into their existing fan base and benefit from their expertise.

5. Leverage Data and Analytics: Utilize YouTube's analytics tools to gain insights into your channel's performance. Analyze viewer demographics, engagement metrics, and watch time to identify patterns and trends. Use this data to make informed decisions about your content strategy, optimize your videos, and refine your targeting.

As YouTube continues to evolve and shape the digital landscape, it presents immense opportunities for content creators and marketers. By understanding the latest trends, embracing new technologies, and staying ahead of the curve, you can position yourself for success on this dynamic platform. The future of YouTube marketing holds endless possibilities, and by continually adapting and innovating, you can unlock new avenues for growth, engagement, and connection with your audience.

Chapter 11

Your YouTube Marketing Journey Begins!

11.1 Recap of Key Takeaways

Throughout this book, we have explored the power of YouTube as a marketing platform and delved into various strategies for success. As we conclude this journey, let's recap some of the key takeaways to help you embark on your YouTube marketing journey:

1. YouTube's Influence: YouTube has emerged as a dominant force in the digital landscape, with billions of users and countless hours of video content being consumed daily. Understanding the platform's impact and potential is crucial for leveraging it effectively in your marketing efforts.

2. Content Strategy: Developing a well-defined content strategy is essential for success on YouTube. It involves identifying your target audience, understanding their preferences, and creating compelling and valuable content that resonates with them. Consistency, quality, and relevance are the pillars of a strong content strategy.

3. Optimization for Visibility: Optimizing your videos for maximum visibility is critical to attracting and engaging viewers. This includes conducting keyword research, crafting attention-grabbing titles and descriptions, creating compelling thumbnails, and using video tags strategically. Implementing these optimization techniques increases the chances of your videos being discovered and watched.

4. Building a community: Building a strong community around your YouTube channel is a powerful way to foster engagement and loyalty. Encouraging viewer interaction, responding to comments, and collaborating with other creators are effective strategies for nurturing a community and fostering meaningful connections with your audience.

5. Monetization Opportunities: YouTube offers various monetization opportunities, including ads, sponsorships, affiliate marketing, and channel memberships. Understanding the monetization policies and requirements, exploring different revenue streams, and finding the right balance between monetization and maintaining viewer trust are key considerations.

6. Analytics and Insights: Utilizing YouTube's analytics tools provides valuable insights into your channel's performance. Tracking metrics such as watch time, engagement, and audience demographics helps you understand what is resonating with your viewers and make data-driven decisions to optimize your content and strategy.

11.2 Developing Your Action Plan for YouTube Success

Now that you have gained a comprehensive understanding of YouTube marketing, it's time to develop your action plan for success. Here are some steps to guide you:

1. Define Your Goals: Clearly define your goals for YouTube marketing. Whether it's increasing brand awareness, driving website traffic, generating leads, or increasing sales, having well-defined goals will guide your strategy and help you measure success.

2. Know Your Audience: Gain a deep understanding of your target audience on YouTube. Research their interests, preferences, and viewing habits to tailor your content to their needs and preferences effectively.

3. Content Strategy: Develop a content strategy that aligns with your goals and resonates with your target audience. Plan the types of videos you will create, the frequency of uploads, and the themes that will engage your viewers. Consider incorporating a mix of educational, entertaining, and inspiring content to keep your audience engaged.

4. Optimization Techniques: Implement optimization techniques to maximize the visibility of your videos. Conduct keyword research, optimize titles and descriptions, create compelling thumbnails, and use relevant tags to enhance your discoverability.

5. Community Engagement: Foster engagement and build a community around your channel. Encourage viewers to leave comments, respond to their feedback, and create opportunities for interaction. Collaborating with other creators can also help expand your reach and build connections.

6. Monetization Strategy: Explore different monetization opportunities that align with your goals and audience. Whether it's through ads, sponsorships, affiliate marketing, or channel memberships, develop a

monetization strategy that complements your content and enhances your revenue potential.

7. Analytics and Optimization: Continuously analyze your channel's performance using YouTube's analytics tools. Track key metrics, identify trends, and optimize your content and strategy based on the insights you gather. Experiment with different approaches, A/B test your videos, and learn from the data to continually improve and grow.

8. Stay Updated: YouTube is a dynamic platform, and trends and features evolve over time. Stay updated with the latest changes, embrace new technologies and video formats, and adapt your strategy accordingly to stay ahead of the competition.

By following these steps and continuously iterating and improving your approach, you will be well on your way to achieving success on YouTube.

Mastering YouTube marketing requires a combination of creativity, strategy, and continuous learning. This book has provided you with the knowledge and tools to navigate the ever-changing landscape of YouTube marketing. From understanding the platform's power to creating engaging content, optimizing for visibility, building a community, and leveraging monetization opportunities, you now have a solid foundation to start your YouTube marketing journey.

Remember, success on YouTube is a journey, not a destination. It requires dedication, persistence, and a willingness to adapt to the evolving needs and preferences of your audience. Stay focused on your goals, remain authentic, and always strive to provide value to your viewers. With the right mindset and strategic approach, you can unlock the immense potential of YouTube and achieve your marketing objectives.

So, go ahead, take what you've learned, and embark on your YouTube marketing adventure. Your audience is waiting, and the possibilities are endless.

Appendix

Helpful Resources and Tools for YouTube Marketing

YouTube marketing is a dynamic and competitive landscape that requires continuous learning and the use of effective tools and resources. In this appendix, we will explore some valuable resources and tools that can enhance your YouTube marketing efforts.

1. YouTube Analytics and Insights Tools

Understanding the performance of your YouTube channel and individual videos is crucial for optimizing your strategy and achieving success. YouTube provides its own analytics tools that offer valuable insights into your audience, engagement metrics, and video performance. These tools allow you to track key metrics such as views, watch time, likes, comments, and subscriber growth. By analyzing this data, you can gain a deeper understanding of your audience's preferences, identify trends, and make data-driven decisions to improve your content and engagement.

Additionally, there are third-party analytics tools available that provide more advanced insights and features. Tools like TubeBuddy and VidIQ offer detailed analytics, keyword research, competitor analysis, and optimization suggestions to help you maximize your YouTube presence. These tools can provide valuable insights and recommendations for improving your content strategy, optimizing video metadata, and increasing your channel's visibility.

2. Video Editing Software and Tools

Creating visually appealing and professionally edited videos is essential for capturing and retaining viewers' attention on YouTube. There are various video editing software and tools available that cater to different skill levels and budgets.

For beginners, simple and user-friendly tools like iMovie (for Mac) and Windows Movie Maker (for Windows) provide basic editing features, allowing you to trim, cut, and add basic effects to your videos. These tools are a great starting point for those new to video editing.

If you're looking for more advanced editing capabilities, software like Adobe Premiere Pro and Final Cut Pro X offer a wide range of features, including advanced effects, transitions, color correction, and audio editing. These professional-grade tools provide greater flexibility and creative control over your videos.

In addition to desktop software, there are also online video editing platforms like WeVideo and Clipchamp that allow you to edit videos directly in your web browser. These platforms offer a range of editing features and are convenient for quick edits or when you don't have access to a desktop editing software.

3. Keyword Research Tools for YouTube SEO

Keyword research is crucial for optimizing your YouTube videos and improving their discoverability in search results. Understanding what keywords and phrases your target audience is using to search for content on YouTube can help you create relevant and optimized video titles, descriptions, and tags.

YouTube's own search suggest feature is a valuable resource for finding popular keywords. As you type in the YouTube search bar, it provides suggestions based on popular search queries. Pay attention to these suggestions as they reflect what people are actively searching for on the platform.

In addition to YouTube's search suggest feature, there are third-party keyword research tools specifically designed for YouTube SEO. Tools like Google Keyword Planner, TubeBuddy's Keyword Explorer, and VidIQ's Keyword Research provide insights into search volume, competition, and related keywords. These tools can help you identify high-traffic keywords and optimize your videos to rank higher in search results.

4. YouTube Channel Management and Optimization Tools

Managing and optimizing your YouTube channel involves various tasks, including scheduling uploads, creating engaging thumbnails, managing comments, and analyzing channel performance. To streamline these processes and maximize efficiency, there are several tools available.

YouTube's Creator Studio provides essential channel management features, including video scheduling, channel customization, comment moderation, and analytics. It's a comprehensive platform for managing your channel's day-to-day operations.

To further enhance your channel management, tools like Hootsuite and Sprout Social allow you to schedule and publish YouTube videos alongside your other social media content. These tools offer a centralized dashboard for managing multiple social media platforms, including YouTube, and provide valuable analytics and reporting features.

When it comes to thumbnail creation, tools like Canva and Adobe Spark offer user-friendly templates and customization options to help you create eye-catching thumbnails that entice viewers to click on your videos. These tools enable you to add text, graphics, and effects to create visually appealing thumbnails that accurately represent your video content.

Conclusion

In the world of YouTube marketing, leveraging the right resources and tools can significantly enhance your efforts and increase your chances of success. The resources and tools mentioned in this appendix provide valuable insights, simplify various tasks, and optimize your YouTube presence.

Remember, while these resources and tools are powerful assets, they are most effective when combined with a solid content strategy, creativity, and a deep understanding of your target audience. Continuously learn and adapt your approach based on the insights and data you gather from these resources.

As you embark on your YouTube marketing journey, make use of these helpful resources and tools to optimize your channel, create engaging videos, and reach your target audience effectively. Stay informed about the latest trends, experiment with different strategies, and always strive for excellence in your YouTube marketing efforts.

Good luck!

Bonus

Introduction to YouTube Automation 2023

In the rapidly evolving landscape of digital marketing, automation has become a game-changer. It has revolutionized various aspects of online business, including social media marketing. One platform that has witnessed significant automation advancements is YouTube. In this bonus chapter, we will explore the concept of YouTube automation and how it can streamline your marketing efforts, save time, and boost your channel's growth in 2023.

1. The Rise of YouTube Automation

YouTube automation refers to the use of automated tools and systems to perform tasks on the platform. It leverages technology and algorithms to streamline processes, optimize performance, and enhance efficiency. With the increasing popularity of YouTube as a marketing channel, automation has become a crucial strategy for content creators and businesses alike.

2. Benefits of YouTube Automation

2.1 Time-Saving: One of the primary benefits of YouTube automation is the significant amount of time it can save. By automating repetitive tasks such as video uploading, thumbnail creation, and metadata optimization, you can focus more on content creation and strategic planning.

2.2 Consistency and Efficiency: Automation ensures consistent branding and messaging across your YouTube channel. It helps maintain a regular upload schedule, ensures optimized metadata for each video, and enhances the overall efficiency of your channel management.

2.3 Improved SEO: YouTube automation tools can assist in keyword research, suggest relevant tags, and optimize video descriptions. These features help improve the search engine optimization (SEO) of your videos, increasing their visibility and organic reach.

2.4 Audience Engagement: Automation can also be utilized to engage with your audience more effectively. Automated comment moderation filters out spam or inappropriate comments, ensuring a positive user experience. Additionally, automated responses to frequently asked questions can save time while maintaining engagement.

3. YouTube Automation Tools and Features

3.1 Video Upload Automation: Tools like TubeBuddy and VidIQ offer features that allow you to schedule and automate video uploads. You can pre-plan and upload multiple videos at once, specifying the date and time for each video to go live.

3.2 Thumbnail Generation: Automated thumbnail generation tools utilize artificial intelligence (AI) algorithms to suggest or create thumbnails based on your video content. These tools analyze your video and generate appealing thumbnails that capture the attention of potential viewers.

3.3 Metadata Optimization: Automation tools provide suggestions for video titles, descriptions, and tags based on keyword research. This streamlines the process of optimizing your video metadata for better search rankings and visibility.

3.4 Comment Moderation: Automating comment moderation helps filter out spam or inappropriate comments, ensuring a safe and positive environment for your audience. Tools like YouTube Studio offer features to automatically hold, hide, or flag certain types of comments.

3.5 Analytics and Reporting: Automation tools provide in-depth analytics and reporting features that help track the performance of your YouTube channel and individual videos. These insights enable data-driven decision-making and help optimize your content strategy.

4. The Future of YouTube Automation

As technology continues to advance, the capabilities of YouTube automation are expected to expand. Artificial intelligence and machine learning algorithms will play a significant role in enhancing automation features, such as more advanced video analysis for thumbnail generation and content recommendation systems.

Additionally, integration with other automation platforms and technologies, such as social media management tools and customer relationship management (CRM) systems, will enable seamless cross-platform automation and data synchronization.

However, it's important to note that while automation can streamline processes and enhance efficiency, it should not replace human creativity and personalization. Balancing automation with authentic, high-quality content creation is crucial for long-term success on YouTube.

YouTube automation has emerged as a powerful strategy for content creators and businesses to optimize their marketing efforts on the platform. With its time-saving capabilities, improved efficiency, and audience engagement features, automation can be a game-changer in maximizing the growth and success of your YouTube channel in 2023.

By leveraging the right automation tools and features, you can streamline your workflow, maintain consistency, and improve your channel's performance. However, it's important to strike a balance between automation and maintaining a personal touch in your content to ensure authenticity and resonate with your audience.

As you venture into YouTube automation, stay informed about the latest trends and advancements, experiment with different tools, and continuously adapt your strategy based on data-driven insights. Embrace the power of automation to amplify your YouTube marketing efforts and make the most out of this dynamic platform in 2023 and beyond.

Printed in Great Britain
by Amazon

37487739R00051